JOURNAL

loved
JOURNAL

women of faith™ | TYNDALE® MOMENTUM

An Imprint of
Tyndale House Publishers, Inc.

Visit Women of Faith at www.womenoffaith.com.

Visit Tyndale online at www.tyndale.com.

Visit Tyndale Momentum online at www.tyndalemomentum.com.

TYNDALE, Tyndale Momentum, and the Tyndale Momentum logo are registered trademarks of Tyndale House Publishers, Inc. Tyndale Momentum is an imprint of Tyndale House Publishers, Inc., Carol Stream, Illinois. *Women of Faith* is a trademark of Women of Faith LLC.

Loved Journal

Designed by Stephen Vosloo

Scripture quotations are taken from the *Holy Bible,* New Living Translation, copyright © 1996, 2004, 2007, 2013 by Tyndale House Foundation. Used by permission of Tyndale House Publishers, Inc., Carol Stream, Illinois 60188. All rights reserved.

Scripture quotations marked NIV are taken from the Holy Bible, *New International Version,*® *NIV.*® Copyright © 1973, 1978, 1984, 2011 by Biblica, Inc.® Used by permission. All rights reserved worldwide.

Printed in China

ISBN 978-1-4964-0828-0

21 20 19 18 17 16 15
7   6   5   4   3   2   1

Introduction

THIS IS YOUR BOOK.

Not just "yours" in the sense that you own it; yours because the content is completely up to you.

Flip through it and you'll find pages waiting to be filled with whatever inspires you. Write, draw, paste, or tuck something inside—it's completely up to you. No one else will have a book just like yours. It will be unique . . . just as you are.

We've called this journal *Loved* because the word describes you perfectly. You are loved. No matter how you feel on any given day—God loves you, all day, *every* day. As 1 John 3:1 says, "See how very much our Father loves us, for he calls us his children, and that is what we are!" There's quite a bit written about God's love for you in his book, the Bible. You might think of this journal as a place to write your thoughts and prayers back to him.

If you're a seasoned journal writer, we hope you feel comfortable among these pages and are eager to begin filling in all those deliciously blank lines. If you're new to journaling, you may be wondering how to get started. Relax: There's no right or wrong way to go about it. We've included a number of quotes and Scriptures throughout to help spark reflection and personal insights. In addition, you'll find some questions on the next page that may get your creativity flowing. It might help to remember that, unless you choose to share, whatever you put on these pages is a private "conversation" between you and God.

No matter how you choose to use your journal, our hope is that it will remind you—or encourage you to discover for the very first time—what God's grace and love mean for you.

You are seen. You are known. You are free. You are *loved*.

Thought Starters

When did you first realize God loved you?

How have you experienced his love for you this week, this month, this year?

How does the fact that you are loved by God affect the way you relate to other people?

Have you ever felt insignificant? Invisible? You're not! God sees you. Does that thought make you smile or make you nervous? Why is that?

When you think about how much God sees (everything!), does it affect your actions? Your attitude?

What does it mean to be truly known by another?

God knows you inside and out. He created you specifically to be you. How does that make you feel?

What does it mean to experience freedom in your relationship with Christ?

What does the Bible say about freedom? What do you think that looks like for you?

Are there places and spaces in your life where you want to enjoy greater freedom than you feel now? What's holding you back?

If you were going to write a letter to God, what would it say? How do you think he would respond to you?

Get quiet, get in position, get focused, and then get ready for one of the greatest experiences of your life: communication with the God of everything, who knows and sees everything and who wants to tell you something!

THELMA WELLS

God's truth is true no matter what is
going on in the world around us.

SHEILA WALSH

♡

_____

_____

_____

_____

_____

_____

_____

_____

_____

_____

_____

_____

_____

_____

*Start where you are and see where God
takes you. Remember: wherever God has you
today, he will be faithful to use you.*

MARY GRAHAM

What you think is based on reasoning.
What you believe is based on truth.

MARILYN MEBERG

♡

_You saw me before I was born. Every day of my
life was recorded in your book. Every moment
was laid out before a single day had passed._

PSALM 139:16

Now all glory to God, who is able, through his
mighty power at work within us, to accomplish
infinitely more than we might ask or think.

EPHESIANS 3:20

_____

_____

_____

_____

_____

_____

_____

_____

_____

_____

_____

_____

_____

_____

_____

_____

_____

♡

♡

How would you love if you weren't afraid?

LISA BEVERE

You can rest assured that nothing that is for you will slip past you. Show up, do good work, trust God for the increase.

ANITA RENFROE

_____

_____

_____

_____

_____

_____

_____

_____

_____

_____

_____

_____

_____

_____

Nothing is going to change around us
unless it's changed within us.

CHRISTINE CAINE

When you are down to nothing,
God is up to something.

BABBIE MASON

_You are good at something for a reason. God designed
you this way; this is on purpose. It isn't fake or a
fluke or small. These are the mind and heart and
hands and voice you've been given:_ Use them.

JEN HATMAKER

Now I am giving you a new commandment: Love each other. Just as I have loved you, you should love each other.

JOHN 13:34

♡

*Even when you don't have the time or opportunity
to speak a word for Christ, you can still do this:
You can spend time in His presence, soaking up His
light, and then allow that light to shine in whatever
dark or uncertain situation you find yourself.*

JONI EARECKSON TADA

God doesn't love me because he's good; he loves me because he's merciful. He loves me even on my worst day.

LISA HARPER

♡

*Don't miss the surprises in life. Pay attention
to the little things God does . . . especially those
for which you've never asked. Then thank
Him and tell somebody what He's done.*

LUCI SWINDOLL

God is always with you, which actually would be frightening except he is with you. He is for you. He loves you. He goes where you go.

LIZ CURTIS HIGGS

_____

_____

_____

_____

_____

_____

_____

_____

_____

_____

_____

_____

_____

_____

_____

Why were we born? We were born to be
loved by God! Plain and simple!

MARILYN MEBERG

You are more than you know.

PATSY CLAIRMONT

♡

I will be glad and rejoice in your unfailing
love, for you have seen my troubles, and you
care about the anguish of my soul.

PSALM 31:7

Even Jesus, in his darkest moments in Gethsemane's garden, confessed the need to have his friends nearby. If God's Son needed friends during his hour of crisis, who are we to think that we may be above needing others?

SANDI PATTY

*To pray is to say that there is more than
I can see, and more than I can do. There
is more going on than meets the eye.*

SHAUNA NIEQUIST

Just as you are right now, you are totally loved by our Father. There is nothing you did to earn it. There is nothing you can do to change it. All we can do is run to it and allow our Father to embrace us.

SHEILA WALSH

♡

The LORD your God is living among you. He is
a mighty savior. He will take delight in you with
gladness. With his love, he will calm all your fears.
He will rejoice over you with joyful songs.

ZEPHANIAH 3:17

Poetry is one of the best ways I have found to get at the deepest feelings buried in those layers. When I meet the page as a poet, I don't write in complete sentences, and my words don't even have to make any sense to anyone. That sets me free to write the truth of what I know, and leave gaps where I have questions or confusion.

NICOLE JOHNSON

♡

Isn't it a wonderful thing that God never runs out
of anything; He has an abundance of everything!

LUCI SWINDOLL

The real tragedy is not to have a broken heart,
but to have a heart that's unbreakable.

LISA HARPER

Let your light shine for all to see. For the glory
of the LORD rises to shine on you.

ISAIAH 60:1

There is nothing more liberating than
being fully known and still loved.

MARILYN MEBERG

_____

_____

_____

_____

_____

_____

_____

_____

_____

_____

_____

_____

_____

Look around you for the blessings God is showering
upon you as He affirms His love for you today.

Sandi Patty

[God] seems to delight in using the unexpected,
the least likely, or the weakest link to turn our lives
upside down and inside out . . . and fulfill the plan
he has had in mind since the beginning of time.

THELMA WELLS

God does not exist just to make our lives better;
we exist so that we can learn to love and
worship Him in spirit and in truth.

SHEILA WALSH

God—the God of the universe; the God of heaven and earth; the almighty, awesome, amazing God—knows my name. And he knows you, and he calls you by name. By his spirit and through the majesty of his grace, you are his.

MARY GRAHAM

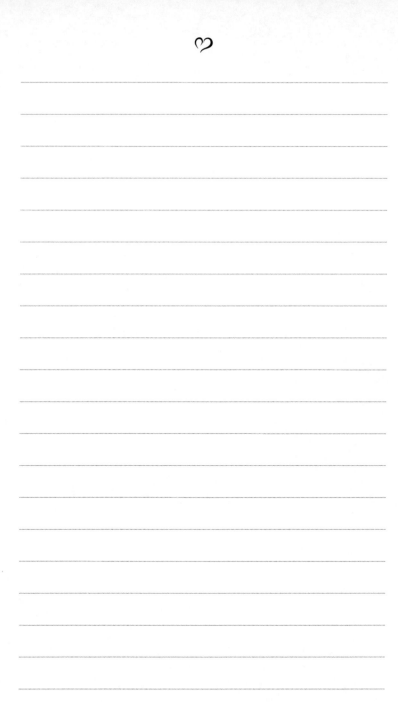

*When we look God right in the eye with
sincerity, gathering as near Him as possible, we
notice it makes a big difference in the outcome
of our day. Our week. Even our lives.*

Luci Swindoll

Whether you feel like the top dog or the runt of the litter, you are loved. As you are right now, with everything that feels right about your life and everything that feels wrong, you are loved. That has to be enough to make you want to wag your tail!

SHEILA WALSH

♡

You and I have been created by God and destined by him to transform the world around us. Our world is full of darkness, hopelessness, and loneliness . . . but you and I are an answer to someone else's prayer.

CHRISTINE CAINE

*Your mind can be a factory of fear or a
fountain of faith. It's your decision.*

PATSY CLAIRMONT

I don't know what you are facing today, but my prayer for you is that you will surrender your "What ifs" to our Father in heaven and allow Him to bring peace and grace and laughter to your "What is."

Sheila Walsh

When He is in control of your life, nothing can come between you and God's great plan for you. Not people. Not things. Not slipups, setbacks, or near misses. Nothing can keep God's great plan for you from coming to pass.

BABBIE MASON

The attacks on your life have more to do
with who you can be in the future than who
you were in the past. Will you fight?

LISA BEVERE

*Prayer creates the possibility for internal calm
even in the midst of external chaos.*

SHAUNA NIEQUIST

♡

You've got a part to play on this planet. You're not just taking up space: you're in your city for a reason, you're in your town for a reason, your job for a reason, your school for a reason. Your GPS says "you are here."

CHRISTINE CAINE

God has got your back. He is willing to work alongside of you as you grow and become the woman God has called you to be.

PRISCILLA SHIRER

♡

♡

Whatever you are facing today remember that
God loves you more than you could begin to grasp.
You are welcomed into His presence; just come
as you are. You can even bring your coffee!

SHEILA WALSH

I don't know what is going on in your corner of the world, but I know the One who does. Christ is in the midst of disaster, death, and gratefully, even the daily events of our unfolding lives. We who have invited Christ into our shell-shocked hearts are never, never, no never alone.

PATSY CLAIRMONT

♡

Trust in the LORD with all your heart; do not depend on your own understanding. Seek his will in all you do, and he will show you which path to take.

PROVERBS 3:5-6

Take time to hear the adventures of others—it will help color your imagination. And don't miss the excitement twirling around your own life circle. I figure if God has gone to the artistic effort of painting those lines down the squirming chipmunk's back, put poetry into the deer's flight and music into geese, then I don't want to miss the wonder of it all. And funny thing: Every time I observe His creation I feel richer for it . . . like a queen with her very own palace.

PATSY CLAIRMONT

♡

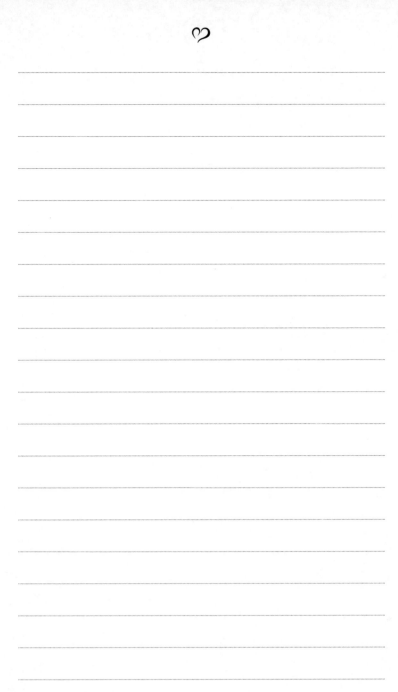

I don't know the origin of the saying "variety is the spice of life," but I wholeheartedly agree with it. I have a feeling God does too because variety is always happening. He's in charge of what's happening . . . so maybe we ought to relax and just "go with the flow."

MARILYN MEBERG

God is bigger than the world. His church is going to arise. This is what we're here for. Nothing changed. Last time I checked theologically, God is still on the throne.

CHRISTINE CAINE

♡

_____

_____

_____

_____

_____

_____

_____

_____

_____

_____

_____

_____

*If we keep recognizing who God is and
being witnesses to what God is doing—
it changes things. It changes us.*

LISA HARPER

We consider our flops or hard times a defeat, but in reality they are God's greatest compliments. They're transforming love gifts from a gracious heavenly Father.

LUCI SWINDOLL

♡

_____

_____

_____

_____

_____

_____

_____

_____

_____

_____

_____

_____

_____

*Don't allow your lack of credentials to
keep you from doing and entering in to the
fullness of what God has for you.*

PATSY CLAIRMONT

Jeremiah 29:11 says that he knows the plans he has for us and that those plans are to give us a hope and a future. Hold on to your dreams, girl—and know that, even though you may have to wait awhile for them to come to pass, you sure do appreciate them all the more when they do.

ANITA RENFROE

♡

_____

_____

_____

_____

_____

_____

_____

_____

_____

_____

_____

_____

_____

_____

_____

*The Shepherd does not allow the sheep to wander or
get lost without going and searching for them.*

MARILYN MEBERG

When I feel frozen in my failure, I just try to imagine my Father running down the road to meet me. I look in his eyes—brimming with acceptance—and remember that it isn't about my failures, it is about his love. It is about being God's beloved daughter, who is always welcome home.

SANDI PATTY

_I can't find anywhere in the Word of God where
it says a woman should get her sense of security,
worth, or value from a place, possession, position,
or any person other than the Lord Jesus Christ._

PATSY CLAIRMONT

Look around your circle of friends today and see if there's somebody who needs a little touch of comfort—a welcoming hug, a listening ear, an invitation to your party— then give it to them. They'll appreciate your kindness, and it just might be the first time in months they've felt comfortable . . . all because of your generous heart.

LUCI SWINDOLL

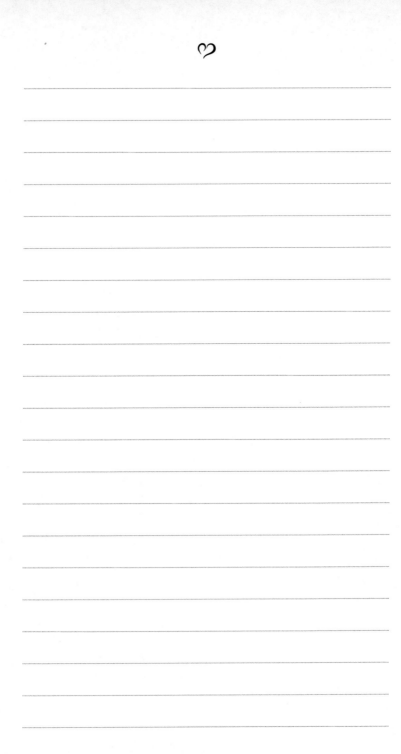

Don't allow what has been done to you to be
bigger than what Jesus has done for you.

CHRISTINE CAINE

Believe it or not, God can still change us.
Not just our habits but our hearts.

JEN HATMAKER

When you have done everything you know to do,
stand and watch for the deliverance of the Lord!

SHEILA WALSH

Wherever you are now is God's provision, not
His punishment. Celebrate this moment and try
very hard to do it with conscious gratitude.

LUCI SWINDOLL

_____

_____

_____

_____

_____

_____

_____

_____

_____

_____

_____

_____

_____

♡

Now may our Lord Jesus Christ himself and God
our Father, who loved us and by his grace gave us
eternal comfort and a wonderful hope, comfort you and
strengthen you in every good thing you do and say.

2 THESSALONIANS 2:16-17

We can't always withdraw to quiet hillsides to pray, but Christ will meet with us in the quiet places of our hearts.

SHEILA WALSH

♡

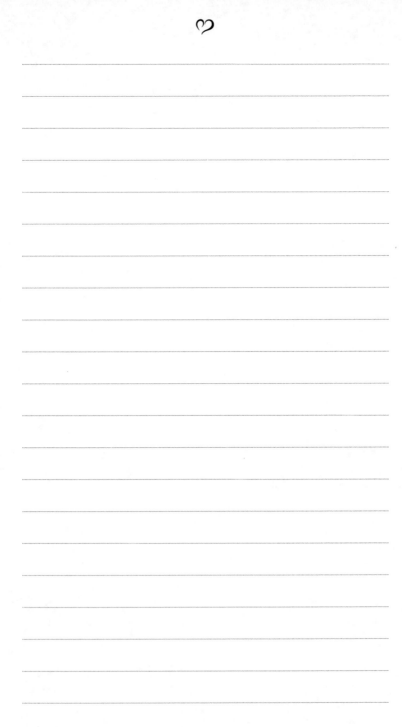

God wants us to serve his purpose on the earth and to
live with him forever when we die. That's the freedom
he gave us on the morning he arose from the grave.

THELMA WELLS

If you're a critic, you can stare and find something wrong. If you're an artist, you can stare and find beauty. God, give me artist's eyes.

ANITA RENFROE

♡

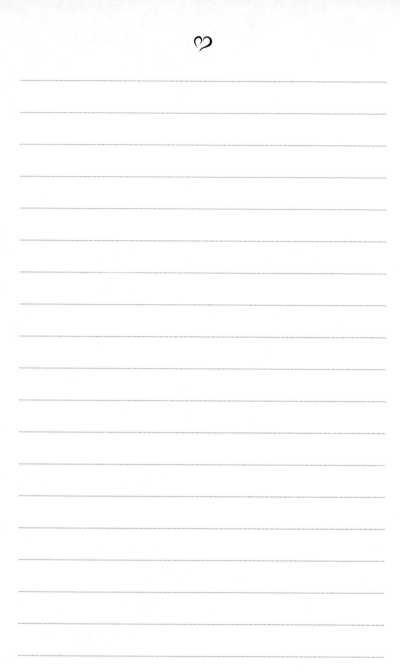

You're still here. You're still alive. You're still
fighting. There's still hope, there's still a destiny,
there's still a future. Do. Not. Give. Up.

CHRISTINE CAINE

God knows all about you; and He loves you—totally,
completely, passionately, boundlessly. Forever.

SHEILA WALSH

When you go to God, He will infuse you
with the strength you need to do that
which He has asked you to do.

PATSY CLAIRMONT

Be on guard. Stand firm in the faith. Be courageous.
Be strong. And do everything with love.

1 CORINTHIANS 16:13-14

♡

*Once you begin to get that God loves you even though
he knows all your mistakes, you can't help but extend
a measure of that grace to people around you.*

LISA HARPER

Choose love—you'll regret mean words,
but never laughter or hugs!

LISA BEVERE

♡

_____

_____

_____

_____

_____

_____

_____

_____

_____

_____

_____

_____

_____

*Give thanks to the L*ORD*, for he is good!*

His faithful love endures forever.

1 Chronicles 16:34

*Sometimes people fail each other. The one who
did not nor ever will fail us is Jesus.*

MARILYN MEBERG

♡

Jesus knows everything that is true about
you . . . and He still loves you.

SHEILA WALSH

The faithful love of the LORD never ends! His mercies never cease. Great is his faithfulness; his mercies begin afresh each morning.

LAMENTATIONS 3:22-23

♡

God's not looking for perfect people,
just available people.

CHRISTINE CAINE

You don't need to be better; you just need to have a better view of who your God is and what He's capable of doing in your life.

PRISCILLA SHIRER

God is our refuge and strength, always
ready to help in times of trouble.

PSALM 46:1

If you are in a good season, enjoy and celebrate it. If you are in a difficult season, hang on . . . it will change! Ecclesiastes 3:1 says, "There is a time for everything, and a season for every activity under the heavens" (NIV).

SANDI PATTY

_____

_____

_____

_____

_____

_____

_____

_____

_____

_____

_____

_____

If you need greater clarification in your life,
if you're uncertain what next step you should
take . . . then invite Christ to bring the light of
His life into your darkened understanding.

PATSY CLAIRMONT

Whether you win or lose, whether you have a good day or bad day, God is with you; He loves you.

LUCI SWINDOLL

_____

_____

_____

_____

_____

_____

_____

_____

_____

_____

_____

_____

_____

*This is how God loved the world: He gave his
one and only Son, so that everyone who believes
in him will not perish but have eternal life.*

JOHN 3:16

Have the courage to step up and
into the purposes of God.

CHRISTINE CAINE

How great you are, O Sovereign LORD!
There is no one like you. We have never
even heard of another God like you!

2 SAMUEL 7:22

God showed how much he loved us by sending his one and only Son into the world so that we might have eternal life through him.

1 JOHN 4:9

The Bible is true, no matter how contrary to
reality it appears. I've discovered you can press
extremely hard on the Word, and it will hold.

JEN HATMAKER

Interrupt your day with little celebrations. Your real life will all be waiting for you when you're done and nothing will be all that different. But you will.

LUCI SWINDOLL

Your past does not determine your future;
Jesus Christ does.

SHEILA WALSH

Dear friends, since God loved us that much,
we surely ought to love each other.

1 JOHN 4:11

Sometimes all you can do is
begin again. Again. Again.

SHAUNA NIEQUIST

Do not be afraid or discouraged, for the LORD *will personally go ahead of you. He will be with you; he will neither fail you nor abandon you.*

DEUTERONOMY 31:8

_____

_____

_____

_____

_____

_____

_____

_____

_____

_____

_____

_____

_____

_____

_____

*The most difficult time in your life may
be the border to your promised land.*

CHRISTINE CAINE

Long ago the LORD said to Israel: "I have loved you,
my people, with an everlasting love. With
unfailing love I have drawn you to myself."

JEREMIAH 31:3

_Give yourself to laughter. Take time to
turn your respectable, ordinary, everyday,
commonplace life into the unforgettable happiness
of the moment. You'll never regret it._

LUCI SWINDOLL

Who you are is not the sum of the wrong you've done. Who you are is who God says you are.

SANDI PATTY

♡

This is real love—not that we loved God,

but that he loved us and sent his Son as

a sacrifice to take away our sins.

1 John 4:10

The Word of God has changed me, rearranged me.
The Word gets in you at the cellular level and recreates
you. It makes you new from the inside out.

LIZ CURTIS HIGGS

♡

Your life is God's story being told and His character being displayed. So how does it read? What does it tell others about the God you serve? Will you dare to believe there's a message in this mess? It's quite possibly the best story some people will ever read.

PRISCILLA SHIRER

Look at God. He created the world in six days and then rested *on the seventh. If God rested, we need to follow his lead.*

Thelma Wells

Jesus cares about your crushed spirit;
He will never leave you nor forsake you.

MARILYN MEBERG

*Your Father knows exactly what you
need even before you ask him!*

MATTHEW 6:8

Quit running toward the mirage of a
perfect life. Run to the perfect Savior!

LISA HARPER

The Spirit of God has made me, and the
breath of the Almighty gives me life.

JOB 33:4

♡

_____

_____

_____

_____

_____

_____

_____

_____

_____

_____

_____

_____

_____

Today has amazing potential depending a great
deal on my willingness to participate in it.

PATSY CLAIRMONT

Impossible is where God starts.

CHRISTINE CAINE

God completes what He begins.

He knows us by name.

LUCI SWINDOLL

Permissions

Our thanks to the following for their kind permission to use their material:

Quotes by Lisa Bevere, Women of Faith events 2012, 2013; Twitter 2014. All rights reserved.

Quotes by Christine Caine, Women of Faith events 2012, 2013, 2014; Women of Faith blog 2013; Women of Faith videos 2013, 2014. All rights reserved.

Quotes by Patsy Clairmont, *Women of Faith Devotional Bible.* Copyright © 2010 by Thomas Nelson, Inc., used under license with Thomas Nelson, a division of HarperCollins Christian Publishing, Inc., www.thomasnelson.com. All rights reserved. Women of Faith event 2014; Women of Faith "From the Porch" newsletter. All rights reserved.

Quotes by Mary Graham, Women of Faith "From the Porch" newsletter. All rights reserved.

Quotes by Lisa Harper, Women of Faith event 2014; Women of Faith video 2012. All rights reserved.

Quotes by Jen Hatmaker, *7: An Experimental Mutiny against Excess.* Copyright © 2012 (Nashville, TN: B&H); jenhatmaker.com. All rights reserved.

You have come to the end of your book—but *not* to the end of your story. We hope your journal experience has brought you confidence that you are truly *Loved*. As you move into your next chapter, we invite you to learn more about God's love for you through additional resources from Women of Faith: *You Are Loved Bible Study: Embracing God's Love for You* and *Loved by God Devotional: 52 Encouraging Reminders That You Are Seen, Known, and Free.* You are welcome to join us in person at a Women of Faith 2015 *Loved* event or to watch the *Loved* DVD (recorded live on the 2015 tour). To learn more, visit us online at WomenofFaith.com.